H[ow to]
START &
MANAGE
YOUR OWN
BUSINESS

MI.0962875902

HOW TO START & MANAGE YOUR OWN BUSINESS

A Practical Way To Start
Your Own Business

By
Jerre G. Lewis
Leslie D. Renn

Lewis & Renn Associates, Inc.
Interlochen, Michigan

*Additional copies of this book may be ordered through
bookstores or by sending $9.95 plus $3.50
for postage and handling to
Publishers Distribution Service
6893 Sullivan Road
Grawn, MI 49637
1-800-507-2665*

Copyright © 1992, 1994 by Jerre G. Lewis and Leslie D. Renn

All rights reserved. No part of this book may be reproduced, by any means, without permission in writing from the publisher, except by a reviewer who wishes to quote brief excerpts in connection with a review in a magazine or newspaper. For information contact, Lewis & Renn Associates, Inc., 10315 Harmony Dr., Interlochen, MI 49643.

Third Printing 1994

Publisher's Cataloging-in-Publication Data

Lewis, Jerre G., 1937-

> How to start and manage your own business : a practical
> way to start your own business / by Jerre G. Lewis and Leslie
> D. Renn—Interlochen, Mich. : Lewis & Renn Associates.
>   p.   cm.
> Includes bibliographical references and index.
> ISBN 0-9628759-0-2
> 1. New business enterprises — Management. 2. Small
> business — Management. I. Renn, Leslie, D., 1940-
> II. Title

HD62.7   1991
658.1'141   91-60125

Manufactured in the United States of America

10 9 8 7 6 5 4 3

Text design by Laura Argyle / PDS

To my wife Victoria, and my children Elizabeth, Marie, John, and Becky Lewis.

To my wife Donna, and my children Leslie, Kevin, Jeffrey, and Christine Renn.

Preface

How To Start and Manage Your Own Business is a text for those men and women who are interested in pursuing the Great American dream of owning their own business. It provides the knowledge and tools necessary to successfully plan, design, and start up a new business. The book is written in such a way that the material can be grasped by practitioners having little or no background in business and is intended to help "study" the start-up process.

There is a resurgence of activity in new ventures in the United States today. Even large companies are getting into the act, trying to figure out how to encourage the innovation and commitment that entrepreneurial activity seems to engender. The vast majority of new small companies are the result of the effort of just plain people. For such individual entrepreneurs, there has been generally little formal assistance. This book was written, in fact, to help fill that gap.

The United States has developed into an entrepreneurial economy, and the creation of new ventures is at the center of the activity. New enterprises are being developed at a record pace. Successful entrepreneurship requires more than merely luck and money. It is a cohesive process of creativity, risk-taking and planning. This book is a step-by-step guide to start and manage your own business in an easy-to-read and easy-to-understand format.

Small business provides unbounded opportunities for individuals to pursue dreams of independence and financial success. Follow these guidelines and achieve your goals and dreams.

Contents

How To
Start &
Manage
Your Own
Business

Chapter 1

Introduction

Selecting the right business opportunity requires careful, thorough evaluations of yourself, the type of business you would like to operate in your desired area, and those businesses that meet your needs and expectations. Owning your own business is as much a part of the American dream as owning a home, and for you, this urge represents one of life's most exciting challenges. This book is for those men and women who someday may go into business for themselves and for those who are already in business for themselves but who wish to strengthen their entrepreneurial and managerial skills.

Entrepreneurs come in all shapes and sizes, personalities, and life-styles. They are usually highly motivated, hard-working individuals who receive satisfaction from taking risks. Your business should interest you, not just be an income generator. Analyze your personal style. Do you like working with people? Are you a self starter, goal oriented, persistent, a risk taker, willing to work hard and long hours?

If you have been honest in evaluating yourself, you will now select the right type of business. Before you can determine which of the multitude of businesses is right for you to start, you must evaluate the businesses you want to start by asking these questions. Is the business area growing? How does the economy affect it? Who dominates it's markets? Once you have considered a business that satisfies your needs and interest you must prepare a formal business plan by following the outline given in this book.

Small businesses constitute a dynamic and critical sector of the U.S. economy. Every year in the United States more than 600,000 new businesses are launched by independent men and women eager to make their own decisions, express their own ideas, and be their own bosses. But running your own business is not as easy as it may seem. There can be problems with the inventory, or getting the right goods delivered on time. Yet, managing one's own business can be a personally and financially rewarding experience for an individual strong enough to meet the test. A person with stamina, maturity, and creativity, one who is willing to make sacrifices, may find making a go of a struggling enterprise an exhilarating challenge with many compensations.

4

Small business owners are a dedicated group of people who work hard and whose hours on the job usually exceed the nine-to-five routine. The owner's commitment is the key to many successful small businesses; an entrepreneur is able to communicate ideas, lead, plan, be patient, and work well with people.

Managing a business requires more than the possession of technical knowledge. Because most small businesses are started by technical people, such as engineers and salesmen, their managerial acumen is often less developed than their technical skills. The need to plan for management is common to every type and size of business, and there are certain steps that must be taken. Although some of them are very elementary — such as applying for a city business permit — the most important are often complex and difficult and require the advice of specialists: accountants, attorneys, insurance brokers, and/or bankers. For almost any business though, the first step will be to translate the entrepreneur's basic idea into a concrete plan for action.

First: Am I an entrepreneur?

Should you go into business? Without a clear assessment of the risks and burdens involved, you could be headed for a painful and costly disappointment. Owning your own business means hard work, long hours and for most little financial compensation at first. If you are looking for glamour, security, long lunch hours and regular vacations, you should work for someone else.

To gauge your level of entrepreneurial spirit, the following quiz was created. Please answer each question honestly and then total the columns.

ENTREPRENEURIAL QUIZ

	YES	NO	SOMETIMES
1. I am a self-starter. Nobody has to tell me how to get going.	___	___	_____
2. I am capable of getting along with just about everybody.	___	___	_____
3. I have no trouble getting people to follow my lead.	___	___	_____
4. I like to be in charge of things and see them through.	___	___	_____
5. I always plan ahead before beginning a project. I am usually the one who gets everyone organized.	___	___	_____
6. I have a lot of stamina. I can keep going as long as necessary.	___	___	_____
7. I have no trouble making decisions and can make up my mind in a hurry.	___	___	_____
8. I say exactly what I mean. People can trust me.	___	___	_____
9. Once I make my mind up to do something, nothing can stop me.	___	___	_____
10. I am in excellent health and have a lot of energy.	___	___	_____

	YES	NO	SOMETIMES
11. I have experience or technical knowledge in the business I intend to start.	—	—	————
12. I feel comfortable taking risks if it is something I really believe in.	—	—	————
13. I have good communication skills.	—	—	————
14. I am flexible in my dealings with people and situations.	—	—	————
15. I consider myself creative and resourceful.	—	—	————
16. I can analyze a situation and take steps to correct problems.	—	—	————
17. I think I am capable of maintaining a good working relationship with employees.	—	—	————
18. I am not a dictator. I am willing to listen to employees, customers and suppliers.	—	—	————
19. I am not rigid in my policies. I am willing to adjust to meet the needs of employees, customers, and suppliers.			
20. More than anything else, I want to run my own business.	—	—	————
	—	—	————

Total of Column #1———————
Total of Column #2———————
Total of Column #3———————

If the total of Column #1 is the highest, then you will probably be very successful in running your own business.

If the total of Column #2 is the highest, you may find that running a business is more than you can handle.

If the total of Column #3 is the highest, you should consider taking on a partner who is strong in your weak areas.

NOTE: This quiz was adapted from the Small Business Administration publication "Checklist for Going into Business."

Chapter 2

Planning The Business

Every business begins with an idea—a product to be manufactured or sold, a service to be performed. Whatever the business or its degree of complexity, the prospective business owner needs a comprehensive plan in order to transform a vision into a working operation.

Many small businesses fail because they never had a business plan. Preparing the business plan is an essential first step in starting a firm. This business plan should describe, in writing and in figures, the proposed business and it's products, services, or manufacturing process, it should also include an analysis of the market, a marketing strategy, an organizational plan, and measurable financial objectives. The plan will be used by prospective lenders and investors as a means for evaluating potential success and by the business owner to assess continuously the strength of the operation.

Parts of A Business Plan:

What should a business plan cover? It should be a thorough and objective analysis of both personal abilities and business requirements for a particular product or service. It should define strategies for such functions as marketing and production, organization and legal aspects, accounting and finance. A business plan should answer such questions as:

What do I want and what am I capable of doing?
What are the most workable ways of achieving my goals?
What can I expect in the future?

There is no single best way to begin. What follows is simply a guide and can be changed to suit individual needs.

1. Define long-term goals
2. State short-term
3. Set marketing strategies to meet goals and objectives
4. Analyze available resources
5. Assemble financial data
6. Review plan

Please refer to Figure 2.1 for a complete business plan outline.

The business operator with a realistic plan has the best chance for success.

Figure 2.1

BUSINESS PLAN FOR SMALL BUSINESSES

    I. Type of Business

   II. Location

  III. Target Market

  IV. Planning Process

    V. Organizational Structure

  VI. Staffing Procedures

 VII. Control

VIII. Market Strategy

  IX. Financial Planning

   X. Budgeted Balance Sheet

  XI. Budgeted Income Statement

 XII. Budgeted Cash Flow Statement

XIII. Break-even Chart

Chapter 3

Choosing The Legal Form Of A Business

To begin the actual formation of a new business, the prospective owner might pose the following questions:

How much money do I need?
Where will it come from?
What skills are needed that I cannot provide?
How much control do I want to have over the operation?
How will the business be taxed?

The responses to these questions will strongly influence (and be influenced by) the legal form of the business the prospective owner initially selects. However, the organization of a business is a continuing question, and decisions are based on changing profits and growth of the operation. For instance, the person who starts out as a sole proprietor may at some point lack sufficient capital and seek a partner, or after two or three years of operation, may elect to incorporate. All three forms of business ownership are open to the beginning entrepreneur.

Sole Proprietorship:

The sole proprietorship is by far the most popular form of business ownership. Approximately 75 percent of all businesses in the United States are sole proprietorships. In simple terms, a sole proprietorship is a business owned and managed by one individual. In most states, one has only to obtain the needed local licenses and open for business. The advantages of a sole proprietorship are the simplicity of creation. If you wish to operate under your own name and you have paid all local license fees, you are ready to do business. Sole proprietorship is the least costly form of ownership to start. You do not need to file legal papers as is recommended for a partnership and required for a corporation. The owner has total decision making authority. We have all heard the expression "It's lonely at the top", for the sole proprietor, you are the top. This feature allows the owner to make decisions in a timely manner. See Figure 3.1 for advantages and disadvantages for the sole proprietorship form of business.

Partnership:

A partnership is an association of two or more persons who engage in business as co-owners for the purpose of making a profit. In a partnership, the co-owners (partners) share the assets and the liabilities of the business, and the profits, if any, according to the terms of a contract (partnership agreement) entered into prior to their going into business.

A partnership agreement, or articles of partnership, is not required by law, but it is wise to work with an attorney to develop one that "spells out" the exact status and responsibility of each member in the partnership. All too often the parties think they know what they are agreeing to, only to find later that no real meeting of the minds took place.

The partnership agreement states in writing all of the terms of the partnership:

1. The name of the partnership (name of the business)
2. The place of business (location, address)
3. The purpose of the business
4. The duration of the partnership
5. Who the partners are and their legal addresses
6. Performance by each partner
7. An agreement on how the profits (or losses) will be distributed
8. An agreement on salaries or drawing rights against profits for each partner

9. Partnership dissolution/ending
10. Sale of partnership interest

When a partnership agreement does not exist, the courts will be forced to assign an equal share of the profits or assets to each partner if the business is dissolved. See Figure 3.1 for the advantages and disadvantages of the partnership form of business.

Figure 3.1

LEGAL FORM OF BUSINESS

Sole Proprietorship:

Advantages:
1. Simple to Start
2. All profits to owner
3. Owner in direct control
4. Easy entry and exit
5. Taxed as individual

Disadvantages:
1. Unlimited liability
2. "Jack-of-all-trades"
3. Capital requirement limited
4. Limited life
5. Employee turn-over

Partnership:

Advantages:
1. Easy to originate
2. Credit rating
3. Talent combination
4. Legal contract

Disadvantages:
1. Unlimited liability
2. Misunderstandings
3. Partner withdrawal
4. Regulations

Corporation:

Advantages:
1. Limited liability
2. Expansion potential
3. Transfer of ownership
4. Retain employees

Disadvantages:
1. Double taxation
2. Charter restrictions
3. Employee motivation
4. Legal regulations

Corporation:

"A corporation is an artificial being, invisible, intangible, and existing only in contemplation of the law," wrote Chief Justice John Marshall. In other words, the corporation exists as a separate entity apart from its owners, the shareholders. It makes contracts; it is liable; it pays taxes. It is a "legal person".

The corporation is the most complex of the three major forms of business ownership. The corporation stands as a separate legal entity in the eyes of the law. The life of the corporation is independent of the owners' lives. Because the owners, called shareholders, are legally separate from the corporation, they can sell their interests in the business without affecting the continuation of the business. When a corporation is founded, it accepts the regulations and restrictions placed on it by the state in which it is incorporated and any other state in which it chooses to do business. Generally, the corporation must report it's financial operations to the state's attorney general on an annual basis.

Incorporation can be costly. A corporation must file articles of incorporation with the Secretary of State and in the counties in which it's principal offices are located and/or real estate is held. It is advisable to obtain the services of an attorney to help clarify the many technical aspects of incorporation and other legal matters of a business corporation.

See Figure 3.1 for the advantages and disadvantages of the corporation form of business.

CERTIFICATE OF INCORPORATION

Generally, the first step in the required procedure is preparation, by the incorporators, of a "Certificate of Incorporation." Most states used to require that the certificate be prepared by three or more legally qualified persons, but the modern trend is to require only one incorporator. An incorporator may, but not necessarily must, be an individual who will ultimately own stock in the corporation.

For purposes of expediting the filing of articles, "Dummy" incorporators are often employed. These dummy incorporators are usually associated with a company that performs this service or with an attorney for the organizers. They typically elect their successors and resign at the meeting of the incorporators.

19

Many states have a standard certificate of incorporation form which may be used by small businesses. Copies of this form may be obtained from the designated state official who grants charters and, in some states, from local stationers as well. The following information is usually required:

1. The corporate name of the company. Legal requirements generally are (A) that the name chosen must not be so similar to the name of any other corporation authorized to do business in the state as to lead to confusion and (B) that the name chosen must not be deceptive so as to mislead the public. In order to be sure that the name you select is suitable, check out the availability of the name through the designated state official in each state in which you intend to do business before drawing up a Certificate of Incorporation. This check can be made through a service company. In some states, there is a procedure for reserving a name.

2. Purposes for which corporation is formed. Several states permit very broad language, such as "The purpose of the corporation is to engage in any lawful act or activity for which corporations may be organized." However, most states require more specific language in

setting forth the purposes of the corporation. Even where state law does not require it, the better practice is to employ a "specific object" clause which spells out in broad descriptive terms the projected business enterprise, at the same time taking care to allow for the possibility of territorial, market, or product expansion. In other words, the language should be broad enough to allow for expansion and yet specific enough to convey a clear idea of the projected enterprise.

The use of a specific object clause, even where not required by state law, is advisable for several reasons. It will convey to financial institutions a clearer picture of the corporate enterprise and will prevent problems in qualifying the corporation to do business in other jurisdictions. Reference books or certificates of existing corporations can provide examples of such clauses.

3. Length of time for which the corporation is being formed. This may be a period of years or may be perpetual.

4. Names and addresses of the incorporators. In certain states one or more of the incorporators is required to be a resident of the state within which the corporation is being organized.

5. Location of the registered office of the corporation in the state of incorporation. If you decide to obtain your charter from another state, you will be required to have an office there. However, instead of establishing an office, you may appoint an agent in that state to act for you. The agent will be required only to represent the corporation, to maintain a duplicate list of stockholders, and to receive or reply to suits brought against the corporation in the state of incorporation.

6. Maximum amount and type of capital stock which the corporation wishes authorization to issue. The proposed capital structure of the corporation should be set forth, including the number and classification of shares and the rights, preferences, and limitations of each class of shares.

7. Capital required at time of incorporation. Some states require that a specified percentage of the par value of the capital stock be paid in cash and banked to the credit of the corporation before the certificate of corporation is submitted to the designated state official for approval.

8. Provision for preemptive rights, if any, to be granted to the stockholders and restrictions, if any, on the transfer of shares.

9. Provision for regulation of the internal affairs of the corporation.

10. Names and addresses of persons who will serve as directors until the first meeting of stockholders or until their successors are elected and qualify.

11. The right to amend, alter, or repeal any provision contained in the Certificate of Incorporation. This right is generally statutory, reserved to a majority or two-thirds of the stockholders. Still, it is customary to make it clear in the certificate.

   If the designated state official determines that the name of the proposed corporation is satisfactory, that the certificate contains the necessary information and has been properly executed, and that there is nothing in the certificate or in the corporation's proposed activities that violates state law or public policy, the charter will be issued.

Chapter 4

Marketing The Business

As a potential small business owner, it is important to learn all you can about marketing. You will need to know how to identify your market and how to market your product or service.

As a business person who looks for a profit from the sale of goods, you recognize that without people who want to buy, there is no demand for the things you want to sell. Thus, it is important that, in addition to knowing about the functions of marketing, you also study the activities that will influence the consumer. When you satisfy the specific needs and wants of the customer, then he or she may be willing to pay you a price that will include a profit for you — and to make a profit is one of the reasons you have become a small business owner. Although there are many activities connected with marketing, most of them can be classified in these categories: buy, finance, transport, standardize, store, insure, advertise, and sell.

To market successfully, you should know who your future customers will be. Be as specific as you can about your targeted market. Are you appealing to a specific age range, economic level, or class? Develop a profile of the characteristics of the customers you believe will be most interested in buying your product or service.

Market research is the tool that helps owner/ managers identify potential customers, determine their needs and wants, and ascertain what they are willing to pay. Market research for the small business is generally very informal in nature; it does not need to be sophisticated to be valuable. The process of searching for answers is itself valuable. As with any research, the goal of market research is to reduce the risks associated with making a decision. Questions can be very basic. Such as how many persons of a certain income level live in a specific region. For marketing research to be effective, the following steps must be taken:

1. Determine the specific nature of the problem that needs to be investigated
2. Collect data from whatever sources are available
3. Analyze the data
4. Develop conclusions

You will have to be alert to changing market trends, particularly in an inflationary environment. Is your product or service one that people will eliminate from their budgets if goods and services continue to be increasingly expensive? What are the options and alternatives for your future customers in obtaining your product or service?

What could you do to increase the attractiveness of your products or services so that potential or existing customers will be attracted and held by you. See Figure 4.1 for developing an outline for marketing planning.

Figure 4.1

MARKETING PLANNING

Outline for Marketing:

I. Product/Service Concept:
   a. Name of product or service
   b. Descriptive characteristics of product or service
   c. Unit sales
   d. Analysis of market trends

II. Number of Customers in your Market Area:
   a. Profile of customers
   b. Average customer expenditure
   c. Total market

III. Your Market Potential:
   a. Total market divided by competition
   b. Total market multiplied by percent who will buy your product

IV. Needs of Customers:
   a. Identification
   b. Pleasure
   c. Social approval
   d. Personal interest
   e. Price

V. Direct Marketing Sources:
   a. Trade magazines
   b. Trade associations

c. Small Business Administration (SBA)
d. Government Publications
e. Yellow Pages
f. Marketing directories

VI. Customer Profile:
   a. Geographical
   b. Gender
   c. Age range
   d. Income brackets
   e. Occupation
   f. Educational level

Chapter 5

Managing The Business

Delegating work, responsibility, and authority is difficult in a small business because it means letting others make decisions which involve spending the owner/manager's money. At a minimum, he should delegate enough authority to get the work done, to allow assistants to take initiative, and to keep the operation moving in his absence. Coaching those who carry responsibility and authority in self-improvement is essential and emphasis in allowing competent assistants to perform in their own style rather than insisting that things be done exactly as the owner/manager would personally do them is important. "Let others take care of the details" is the meaning of delegating work and responsibility. In theory, the same principles for getting work done through other people apply whether you have 25 employees and one top assistant or 150 to 200 employees and several keymen yet, putting the principles into practice is often difficult.

Delegation is perhaps the hardest job owner/managers have to learn. Some never do. They insist on handling many details and work themselves into early graves. Others pay lip service to the idea but actually run a one-man shop. They give their assistants many responsibilities but little or no authority. Authority is the fuel that makes the machine go when you delegate work and responsibility. If an owner/manager is to run a successful company, he must delegate authority properly. How much authority is proper depends on your situation. At a minimum, you should delegate enough authority: (1) to get the work done, (2) to allow keymen to take initiative, (3) to keep things going in your absence.

The person who fills a key management spot in the organization must either be a manager or be capable of becoming one. A manager's chief job is to plan, direct, and coordinate the work of others. He should possess the three "I's" - Initiative, Interest, and Imagination. The manager of a department must have enough self-drive to start and keep things moving. Personality traits must be considered. A keyman should be strong-willed enough to overcome opposition when necessary.

When you manage through others, it is essential that you keep control. You do it by holding a subordinate responsible for his actions and checking the results of those actions. In controlling your assistants, try to strike a balance. You should not get into a keyman's operation so closely that you are "in his hair" nor should you be so far removed that you lose control of things.

You need feedback to keep yourself informed. Reports provide a way to get the right kind of feedback at the right time. They can be daily, weekly, or monthly, depending on how soon you need the information. Each department head can report his progress, or lack of it, in the unit of production that is appropriate for his activity; for example, items packed in the shipping room, sales per territory, hours of work per employee.

For the owner/manager, delegation does not end with good control. It involves coaching as well, because management ability is not acquired automatically. You have to teach it. Just as important, you have to keep your managers informed just as you would be if you were doing their jobs.

Part of your job is to see that they get the facts they need for making their decisions. You should be certain that you convey your thinking when you coach your assistants. Sometimes words can be inconsistent with thoughts. Ask questions to make sure that the listener understands your meaning. In other words, delegation can only be effective when you have good communications.

Sometimes an owner/manager finds himself involved in many operational details even though he does everything that is necessary for delegating responsibility. In spite of defining authority, delegating to competent persons, spelling out the delegation, keeping control, and coaching, he is still burdened with detailed work. Usually, he has failed to do one vital thing. He has refused to stand back and let the wheels turn.

If the owner/manager is to make delegation work, he must allow his subordinates freedom to do things their way. He and the company are in trouble if he tries to measure his assistants by whether they do a particular task exactly as he would do it. They should be judged by their results-not their methods. No two persons react exactly the same in every situation. Be prepared to see some action taken differently from the way in which you would do it even though your policies are well defined. Of course, if an assistant strays too far from policy, you need to bring him back in line. You cannot afford second-guessing.

You should also keep in mind that when an owner/manager second-guesses his assistants, he risks destroying their self-confidence. If the assistant does not run his department to your satisfaction and if his shortcomings cannot be overcome, then replace him. But when results prove his effectiveness, it is good practice to avoid picking at each move he makes.

Chapter 6

Selecting A Location

A choice of location should enter early into the new business owner's plans. Site requirements will depend on the type of goods or services to be sold and the market that is sought. For instance, a manufacturing concern must consider proximity to suppliers and customers, available transportation, labor and utility costs, state and local taxes, and regulations.

A retail store owner's primary concerns will be local traffic patterns, parking availability, and neighboring businesses and institutions. All prospective owners should outline their needs - present and future - and then find a location that suits their requirements.

The subject of location is indeed a very large one. A small business owner should distinguish between general location factors and site factors. In this sense, location means the region, the state, the county, or the city which represents the general market area for the planned firm.

The site factors are the particular street, the corner, and the building within the location area. Small business failures often reflect complete neglect of a consideration of specific location factors. Too many small businesses are established in locations because a store space happened to be available for rent. Most students can probably recall a section of their hometowns which became known as the cemetery for small businesses. If the new business planner is not restricted by desire to locate in a particular town or region but is looking for a location anywhere in the country, he can apply all the following general considerations:

1. *Population*: Study the nature of the population in the location site.

2. *Potential Market*: Study your potential market area in terms of the needs and desires of people you want to serve. Are they home owners? Are they renters? Do they live in apartments? What is the age of the population?

3. *Competition*: Know your competition in advance. Check the number of businesses you will be competing against.

4. *Facilities*: Consider the city or town facilities, which include public transportation, banking facilities, civic associations, schools, churches, and professional services clubs.

5. *Parking*: Does the particular site provide an easy parking and access and other comforts for customers?

6. *Surrounding Businesses*: What type of business surrounds the site? It must be recognized that some types of business firms attract customers of one type and others attract other types.

7. *Traffic Density*: What kind of traffic is there at this site, and is it adequate?

8. *Location Factors for Service Businesses*: Locations for service businesses are almost as varied as the types of firms involved, (the beauty shop, TV repair shop, shoe repair shop, etc.). The most important location factor for all service businesses is to know the type of customer to whom you plan to service. With this knowledge, choose a location and site which best fits that customer group.

Finding the right location for your business is crucial to its success or failure. So follow the right steps in selecting a business location.

See Figure 6.1 for Site Selection Criteria.

Figure 6.1

SITE SELECTION CRITERIA

General Questions

- Is the site centrally located to reach my market?
- What is the transportation availability and what are the rates?
- What provisions for future expansion can I make?
- What is the topography of the site (slope and foundation)?
- What is the housing availability for workers and managers?
- What environmental factors (schools, cultural, community atmosphere) might affect my business and my employees?
- What will the quality of this site be in 5 years, 10 years, 25 years?
- What is my estimate of this site in relation to

my major competitor?

- What is the newspaper circulation? Are there concentrations of circulation?
- What other media are available for advertising? How many radio and television stations are there?
- Is the quantity and quality of available labor concentrated in a given area of the city or town? If so, is commuting a way of living in that city or town?
- Is the city centrally located to my suppliers?
- What are the labor conditions, including such things as relationships with the business community and average wages and salaries paid?
- Is the local business climate healthy, or are business failures especially high in the area?
- What about tax requirements? Is there a city business tax? Income tax? What is the property tax rate? Is there a personal property tax? Are there other special taxes?
- Is the available police and fire protection adequate?
- Is the city or town basically well planned and managed in terms of such items as electric power, sewage, and paved streets and sidewalks?

Chapter 7

Promoting The Business

When a new business is opened, the owner must be prepared to publicize the business or its chance for success will be slim. Only a few businesses - such as those with a prime location, nationally known name, or a built-in clientele - can succeed without advertising to promote market awareness and stimulate sales.

The first purpose - promoting customer awareness - applies as much to established businesses as to newcomers.

Whatever your business may be, you will find it easier to retain old customers than to win new ones. When old customers move away from your area, or when their buying needs change, you need new customers to maintain your sales volume. If you expect your business to gain, you will need additional new customers. New customers are those who move into your area or who have grown into your line of products because now they can afford them or they need them. We see advertising and we hear advertising all around us, and yet that is only a part of it. Through advertising, you call the attention of customers to your products.

As a small business owner, you may advertise your business through your location. People pass by and are attracted to your operation because of what you are selling. To get a better idea of what advertising is , consider some of the following functions of advertising:

1. ***To inform:*** Letting customers know what you have for sale through brochures, leaflets, newspapers, radio, TV, and etc..

2. ***Persuade:*** Persuasion is the art of leading individuals to do what you want them to do. There are sales personnel who have persuasive sales presentations, but persuasion in advertising is nonpersonal. The appeal is made through the printed or spoken words or a picture. The influence of an ad on readers occurs as purchasers choose what they want among different products, and different wants. To gain the action you want—a sale—you must persuade a customer to examine personally what you have for sale.

3. ***Reminder:*** Advertising performs its third function when it reminds those who have been persuaded to buy once that the same product will bring satisfaction. The ad will also remind a customer of the characteristics of a product purchased some time ago, and where he or she bought it. Because customers change their loyalty to a place of business, their tastes for products, and often their trading area patronage, advertising is necessary to draw new customers and to hold old customers. To generate results from advertising that will be profitable to your business, you will have to produce answers to the what, where and how of advertising.

What to Advertise:

The nature of your business will partially answer the question "Shall I advertise goods or services?" What are the outstanding features of your business? Is it unique in any way? Doesn't it have strong points? Do you have something to offer that the competition is not able to duplicate? Answers to these questions will give you a start in deciding what to advertise.

Where to Advertise:

Of course, you will want to advertise within your marketing area, however there are a few guidelines to remember:

a. Who are your customers?
b. What is their income range?
c. Why do they buy?
d. How do they buy? Do they pay cash? Charge?
e. What is the radius of your market area?

How to Advertise:

In determining how to advertise, you will have to consider your dollar allocation for advertising and the media suitable to your particular kind of business. However, it is important to have a balance between the presentation of the product or service being advertised and the application of three basic principles.

1. Gain the attention of the audience.
2. Establish a need.
3. Tell where that need may be filled.

See Figure 7.1 for an outline of the different advertising media.

Figure 7.1

ADVERTISING MEDIA

Medium	Market Coverage	Type of Audience
Daily Newspaper	Single Community or entire metro area; zoned editions sometimes available	General
Weekly Newspaper	Single Community	Residents
Telephone Directory	Geographical area or occupational field served by the directory	Active shoppers for goods or services
Direct Mail Audience	Controlled by the advertiser	Controlled
Radio Audience	Definable market area	Selected
Television Audience	Definable market area	Various
Outdoor	Entire metro area	General auto drivers
Magazine	Entire metro area or magazine region	Selected audience

Chapter 8

Financial Planning For Small Businesses

Financial planning is the process of analyzing and monitoring the financial performance of your business so you can assess your current position and anticipate future problem areas. The daily, monthly, seasonal, and yearly operation of your business requires attention to the figures that tell you about the firm's financial health.

Maintaining good financial records is a necessary part of doing business.

The increasing number of government regulations alone makes it virtually impossible to avoid keeping detailed records. Just as important is to keep them for yourself. The success of your business depends on them. An efficient system of recordkeeping can help you to:

- make management decisions
- compete in the marketplace

- monitor performance
- keep track of expenses
- eliminate unprofitable merchandise
- protect your assets
- prepare your financial statements

Financial skills should include understanding of the balance sheet, the profit-and-loss statement, cash flow projection, break-even analysis, and source and application of funds. In many businesses, the husband and wife run the business; it is especially important that both of them understand financial management. Most small business owners are not accountants, but they must understand the tool of financial management if they are going to be able to measure the return on their investment. Although good records are essential to good financial planning, they alone are not enough because their full use requires interpretation and analysis. The owner/manager's financial decisions concerning return on invested funds, approaches to banks, securing greater supplier credit, raising additional equity capital and so forth, can be more successful if he takes the time to develop understanding and use of the balance sheet and profit-and-loss statement.

Balance Sheet:

The balance sheet, Figure 8.1, shows the financial condition of a business at the end of business on a specified day. It is called a balance sheet because the total assets balance with, or are equal to, total liabilities plus owner's capital balance. Current assets are those that the owner does not anticipate holding for long. This category includes cash, finished goods in inventory, and accounts receivable. Fixed assets are long-term assets, including plant and equipment. A third possible category is the intangible asset of goodwill. Liabilities are debts owed by the business, including both accounts payable, which are usually short-term, and notes payable, which are usually long-term debts such as mortgage payments. The difference between the value of the assets and the value of the liabilities is the capital. This category includes funds invested by the owner plus accumulated profits, less withdrawals.

The Income Statement:

This statement, Figure 8.2, is also known as a profit-and-loss (P & L) statement. It shows how a business has performed over a certain period of time. An income statement specifies sales, cost of sales, gross profit, expenses and net income or loss from operations.

Cash-Flow:

Another statement, Figure 8.3, most businesses want is one which explains how they stand on a cash-flow basis, what revenue is coming in from what sources, and how much is going out, for what purposes. The cash-flow statement summarizes and classifies this monetary flow. It is often prepared month by month.

The Break-Even Chart:

Knowing what the total expenses are and how they make a break-even chart, Figure 8.4, are essential to good management. A break-even chart shows the relationship of fixed, variable, and total expenses to sale at all volumes of sales. It measures all expenses and income from sales on the vertical axis, and the units sold or percentage of capacity on the horizontal axis. An accurately drawn break-even chart tells the business owners what sales volumes are necessary to reach the break-even point and the percentage to be derived from any planned expansion of sales. See Figure 8.1 for an outline of a balance sheet, income statement, cash-flow statement, and break-even chart.

Figure 8.1

BALANCE SHEET

	YEAR I	YEAR II
Current Assets		
Cash	$	$
Accounts receivable		
Inventory		
Fixed Assets		
Real estate		
Fixtures and equipment		
Vehicles		
Other Assets		
License		
Goodwill		
TOTAL ASSETS	$	$
Current Liabilities		
Notes payable (due within 1 year)	$	$
Accounts payable		
Accrued expenses		
Taxes owed		
Long-Term Liabilities		
Notes payable (due after 1 year)		
Other		
TOTAL LIABILITIES	$	$
NET WORTH (ASSETS minus LIABILITIES)	$	$

TOTAL LIABILITIES plus NET WORTH should equal ASSETS

Figure 8.2

INCOME STATEMENT

(Name of Business)
INCOME STATEMENT
For the year ending December 31, 19___

OPERATING
RATIOS

A NET SALES
B COST OF GOODS SOLD:
   Inventory Jan. 1
   Purchases
    Less Cash Discount

   Less Inventory Dec. 31
    Cost of Goods Sold
C GROSS PROFIT
D OPERATING EXPENSES:
   Accounting and Legal
   Advertising
   Bad Debts
   Delivery Costs
   Depreciation
   Employee's Wages
   Entertainment and Travel
   Insurance
   Interest
   Maintenance and Repair
   Miscellaneous
   Rent
   Supplies
   Taxes and Licenses
   Utilities and Telephone
   Total Expenses
E NET PROFIT BEFORE OWNER'S
WITHDRAWAL AND INCOME TAXES

DESCRIPTION OF INCOME STATEMENT TERMS

A Net sales: The dollar amount of sales made during the year, excluding sales tax and any returns or allowances.

B Cost of goods sold: The cost value of beginning physical inventory plus merchandise purchased during the year (including freight costs), less discounts received from suppliers, minus the ending physical inventory.

C Gross profit: (Gross Margin) The difference between net sales and cost of goods sold.

D Operating expenses: Including selling, administrative and general overhead costs involved in store operations throughout the year.

E Net profit before owner's withdrawal and income taxes: This is the figure on which the owner will pay income tax and represents his/her compensation.

Figure 8.3

CASH FLOW

		CASH FLOW PROJECTIONS												
	Start-up or prior to loan	Month 1	Month 2	Month 3	Month 4	Month 5	Month 6	Month 7	Month 8	Month 9	Month 10	Month 11	Month 12	TOTAL
Cash (beginning of month)														
Cash on hand														
Cash in bank														
Cash in investments														
Total Cash														
Income (during month)														
Cash sales														
Credit sales payments														
Investment income														
Loans														
Other cash income														
Total Income														
TOTAL CASH AND INCOME														
Expenses (during month)														
Inventory or new material														
Wages (including owner's)														
Taxes														
Equipment expense														
Overhead														
Selling expense														
Transportation														
Loan repayment														
Other cash expenses														
TOTAL EXPENSES														
CASH FLOW EXCESS (end of month)														
CASH FLOW CUMULATIVE (monthly)														

Break-Even Analysis:

The point in the operations of an enterprise at which revenues and expired costs are exactly equal is called the break-even point. At this level of operations an enterprise will neither realize an operating income nor incur an operating loss. Break-even analysis can be applied to past periods, but it is most useful when applied to future periods as a guide to business planning, particularly if either an expansion or a curtailment of operations is anticipated. In such cases it is concerned with future prospects and future operations and hence relies upon estimates. Obviously the reliability of the analysis is greatly influenced by the accuracy of the estimates.

Break-Even Sales (in $) = Fixed Costs (in $) + Variable Costs (as % of Break-Even Sales)

$$S = \$90,000 + 60\% \ S$$
$$40\% \ S = \$90,000$$
$$S = \$225,000$$

A break-even chart, based on the foregoing data, is illustrated on the following page. It is constructed in the following manner:

1. Percentages of productive capacity of the enterprise are spread along the horizontal axis, and the dollar amounts representing

The outside limits of the chart represent 100% of productive capacity and the maximum sales potential at that level of production.

2. A diagonal line representing sales is drawn from the lower left corner to the upper right corner.

3. A point representing fixed costs is plotted on the vertical axis at the left and a point representing total costs at maximum capacity is plotted at the right edge of the chart. A diagonal line representing total costs at various percentages of capacity is then drawn connecting these two points. In the illustration, the fixed costs are $90,000 and the total costs at maximum capacity amount to $330,000 ($90,000 plus variable costs of 60% of $400,000)

4. Horizontal and vertical lines are drawn at the point of intersection of the sales and cost lines, which is the break-even point, and the areas representing operating income and operating loss are identified.

Figure 8.4

BREAK-EVEN CHART

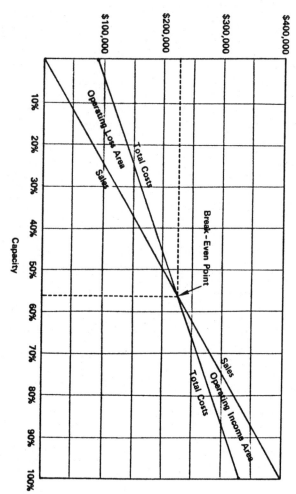

Projected Break-Even Chart
For Year Ending December 31, 19—

Chapter 9

Business References

IRS Publications

15	Employer's Tax Guide Circular E
334	Tax Guide for Small Business
505	Tax Withholding and Estimated Tax
509	Tax Calendar
510	Excise Taxes
533	Self-Employment Tax
535	Business Expenses
552	Recordkeeping Requirements and a List of Tax Publications
583	Information for Business Taxpayers - Business Taxes and Identification
587	Business Use of Your Home
590	Tax Information on Individual Retirement Arrangements
910	Taxpayer's Guide on IRS Information

THESE PUBLICATIONS ARE AVAILABLE ONLY FROM IRS OFFICES.

SBA BUSINESS DEVELOPMENT PAMPHLETS

Financial Management and Analysis
- The ABC's of Borrowing
- Basic Budgets for Profit Planning
- A Venture Capital Primer for Small Business
- Accounting Services for Small Service Firms
- Analyze Your Record to Reduce Cost
- Budgeting in a Small Business Firm
- Sound Cash Management and Borrowing
- Keeping Records in Small Business
- Checklist for Profit Watching
- Simple Break-even Analysis for Small Stores
- A Pricing Checklist for Small Retailers

General Management and Planning
- Locating or Relocating Your Business
- Problems in Managing a Family-Owned Business
- Business Plan for Small Manufacturers
- Business Plan for Small Construction Firms
- Planning and Goal Setting for Small Business
- Fixing Production Mistakes
- Should You Lease or Buy Equipment?
- Checklist for Going Into Business
- Business Plan for Retailers
- Business Plan for Small Service Firms
- Thinking About Going Into Business
- Feasibility Checklist for Starting a
  Small Business of Your Own

- How to Get Started with a Small Business Computer
- The Business Plan for Homebased Business
- Stock Control for Small Stores
- Techniques for Problem Solving
- Techniques for Productivity Improvement
- Selecting the Legal Structure for Your Business
- Evaluating Franchises Opportunities

Crime Prevention
- Reducing Shoplifting Losses
- Preventing Employee Pilferage

Marketing
- Creative Selling: The Competitive Edge
- Is the Independent Sales Agent for You?
- Marketing Checklist for Small Retailers
- Advertising Guidelines for Small Retail Firms
- Plan Your Advertising Budget
- Learning about Your Market
- Selling by Mail Order
- Market Overseas with U.S. Government Help

Personnel Management
- Checklist for Developing a Training Program
- Staffing your Store
- Managing Employee Benefits

New Products, Ideas, and Inventions
- Can You Make Money with your Idea or Invention?
- Introduction to Patents
- Proposal Preparation for Small Business Innovation Research

SBA BUSINESS DEVELOPMENT BOOKLETS

Small Business Management Series
- Cost Accounting for Small Manufacturers
- Handbook of Small Business Finance
- Ratio Analysis for Small Business
- Guides for Profit Planning
- Management Audit for Small Manufacturers
- Insurance and Risk Management for Small Business
- Management Audit for Small Retailers
- Financial Recordkeeping for Small Stores
- Small Store Planning for Growth
- Franchise Index/Profile
- Training Salesmen to Serve Industrial Markets
- Financial Control by Time-Absorption Analysis
- Management Audit for Small Service Firms
- Decision Points in Developing New Products
- Purchasing Management and Inventory Control for Small Business
- Managing the Small Service Firm for Growth and Profit

- Credit and Collection for Small Stores
- Financial Management: How to Make a Go of Your Business

Starting and Managing Series
- Starting and Managing a Small Business of Your Own

Note: For the most up-to-date information concerning publications and videotapes available for starting and managing a successful small business write:

> SBA Publications
> P. O. Box 30
> Denver, Colorado 80201-0030

and ask for The Small Business Directory.

Chapter 10

Franchise Outline

Although the success rate for franchise-owned businesses is significantly better than for many other start-up businesses, success is not guaranteed. One of the biggest mistakes that you can make is to be in a hurry to get into business.

If you shortcut your evaluation of a potential business, you might neglect to consider other franchises that are more suitable for you. Don't be "pressured" into a franchise that is not right for you.

Although most franchises are managed by reputable individuals, as in all industries, some are not. Also, some franchises could be poorly managed and financially weak.

This information will assist you in investigating your options. Questions needed to adequately evaluate the business, the franchisor, the franchise package, and yourself are included.

WHAT IS FRANCHISING?

A franchise is a legal and commercial relationship between the owner of a trademark, service mark, trade name, or advertising symbol and an individual or group seeking the right to use that identification in a business. The franchise governs the method for conducting business between the two parties.

While forms of franchising have been in use since the Civil War, enormous growth has occurred more recently. By the end of 1991, 600,000 establishments in 50 industries will achieve gross sales of over half a trillion dollars and employ 5.6 million full and part-time workers. Industries that rely on franchised business to distribute their products and services touch every aspect of life from automobile sales and real estate to fast foods and tax preparation.

In the simplest form, a franchisor owns the right to a name or trademark and sells that right to a franchise. This is known as "product/trade name franchising". In the more complex form, "business format franchising," a broader and ongoing relationship exists between the two parties.

Business format franchising often provides a full range of services, including site selection, training, product supply, marketing plans, and even financing. Generally, a franchise sells goods or services supplied by the franchisor or sells goods or services that meet the franchisor's quality standards.

BENEFITS OF A FRANCHISE

There are a number of aspects to the franchising method that appeal to prospective business owners. Easy access to an established product as well as a proven method of marketing reduces the many risks of opening a business. In fact S.B.A. and Department of Commerce statistics show a significantly lower failure rate for franchisee-owned businesses than for other business start-ups.

The franchisee purchases, along with a trademark, the experience and expertise of the franchisor's organization. However, a franchise does not ensure easy success.

If you are not prepared for the total commitment of time, energy, and financial resources that any business requires, this is the point at which you should stop.

INVESTIGATE YOUR OPTIONS

As in all major business decisions, nothing substitutes for thorough investigation, planning, and analysis of your options. The following information will help you set up a systematic program to analyze the possibilities and pitfalls of the franchised business you are considering.

Use the questions below to guide your research and cover all the bases. Read the full text before you begin to gather the information you will need.

SOURCES OF INFORMATION

You will need at least the following sources of information as well as experienced professional advice:

A Directory of Franchisors - The Franchise Opportunities Handbook published by the U.S. Department of Commerce is available from:

The Superintendent of Documents
U.S. Government Printing Office
Washington, D.C. 20302.

Others are available at your library.

THE DISCLOSURE DOCUMENT

A Federal Trade Commission rule requires that franchise and business opportunity sellers provide certain information to help you in your decision. The FTC rule requires the franchisor to provide you a detailed disclosure document at least ten days before you pay any money or legally commit yourself to a purchase. This document includes 20 important items of information, such as:

Names, addresses, and telephone numbers of other purchasers.

A fully-audited financial statement of the seller.

The background and experience of the key executives.

The cost required to start and maintain the business.

The responsibilities you and the seller will share once you buy.

CURRENT FRANCHISES

Talk to other owners and ask them about their experiences regarding earnings claims and information in the Disclosure Document. Be certain that you talk to franchisees and not company-owned outlets.

OTHER REFERENCES

You should get more information and publications from the U.S. Small Business Administration, the Federal Trade Commission, the Better Business Bureau, the local Chamber of Commerce and associations, such as:

The International Franchise Assoc.
1025 Connecticut Ave. N.W.
Washington, D.C. 20036.

PROFESSIONAL ADVICE

Finally, unless you have had considerable business experience and legal training, you need a lawyer, an accountant, and a business advisor to counsel you and go over the Disclosure Document and proposed contract. Remember, the money and time you spend before it's too late may save you from a major loss on a bad investment.

WHAT IS THE BUSINESS?

Is the product or service offered new or proven? Is the product one for which you have a solid background? Do you feel a strong motivation for producing the product or providing the service?

Does the product meet a local demand?

Is there a proven market?
What is the competition?

If the product requires servicing, who bears the responsibilities covered by warrantees and guarantees? The franchisee? The franchisor? If neither, are service facilities available?
What reputation does the product enjoy?
Are suppliers available?
What reputation do they enjoy?

WHO IS THE FRANCHISOR?

Visit at least one of the firm's franchisees. Observe the operation and talk to the owner. You need to determine reputation, stability, and financial strength of the franchisor.

How long has the franchisor been in the industry? How long has the firm granted franchises?

How many franchises are there? How many in your area?

Examine the attitude of the franchisor toward you. Is the firm concerned about your qualifications? Are you being rushed to sign the agreement?

Does the firm seem interested in a long-term relationship or does that interest end with the initial fee?

Are you required to purchase supplies from the franchisor? Are the prices competitive with other suppliers?

What, if any, restrictions apply to competition with other franchisees?

What are the terms covering renewal rights? Reselling the franchise?

Again, use your professional support to examine all of these questions. Some of the contract terms may be negotiable. Find out before you sign; otherwise, it will be too late.

PERSONAL ASSESSMENT

Finally, an examination of your own skills, abilities, and experience is perhaps your most important step. Determine exactly what you want out of life and what you are willing to sacrifice to achieve your goals.

Be honest, rigorous, and specific. Ask yourself:

Am I Qualified for this Field?
Physically?
By experience?
By education?
By learning capacity?
Financially?

Ask yourself about the effects of this decision on your family. How will this new life style affect them? Do they understand the risks and sacrifices, and will they support your efforts?

Beginning a franchise business is a major decision that does not ensure easy success. However, an informed commitment of time, energy, and money by you and your family can lead to an exciting and profitable venture.

Chapter 11

Start Your Own Business Guide

A simplified summary of the complete guide to starting and operating a successful business.

A. GET STARTED
 1. Define your educational background and work experience.
 2. Survey all basic types of businesses.
 3. Define what type of business matches your experience and educational background.
 4. Choose only the businesses that you would like to own and operate.
 5. Define what products or services your business will be marketing.
 6. Define who will be using your products/services.
 7. Define why they will be purchasing your products/services.
 8. List all competitors in your market area.

B. WHERE TO START/LOCATION

1. Decide where you want to live.
2. Choose several areas that would match your priorities.
3. Use the list below as a guide to see if your location will match the estimated population needed to support your business.

KIND OF BUSINESS	INHABITANTS PER STORE

FOOD STORES

Grocery Stores	1,534
Meat and Fish (Sea Food) Markets	17,876
Candy, Nut, and Confectionery Stores	31,409
Retail Bakeries	12,563
Dairy Products Stores	41,587

EATING, DRINKING PLACES

Restaurant	1,583
Cafeterias	19,341
Refreshment Places	3,622
Drink Places (Alcoholic beverages)	2,414

GENERAL MERCHANDISE

Variety Stores	10,373
General Merchandise	9,837

APPAREL AND ACCESSORY STORES
Women's Ready-To-Wear Stores	7,102
Women's Accessory and Specialty Stores	25,824
Men's and Boy's Clothing and Furnishing Stores	1,832
Family Clothing Stores	16,890
Shoe Stores	9,350

FURNITURE, HOME FURNISHING, AND EQUIPMENT STORE
Furniture Stores	7,210
Floor Covering Stores	29,543
Drapery, Curtain and Upholstery Stores	62,585
Household Appliance Stores	12,485
Radio and T.V. Stores	20,346
Record Shops	112,144
Musical Instrument Stores	46,332

BUILDING MATERIAL, HARDWARE, AND FARM EQUIPMENT DEALERS
Lumber and other Building Materials Dealers	8,124
Paint, Glass and Wallpaper Stores	22,454
Hardware Stores	10,206
Farm Equipment Dealers	14,793

AUTOMOTIVE DEALERS
Motor Vehicle Dealers
    New and Used Cars   6,000
Motor Vehicle Dealers
    Used Cars Only   17,160
Tire, battery, and Accessory Dealers   8,800

BOAT DEALERS
        61,500

HOUSEHOLD TRAILER DEALERS
        44,746

GASOLINE SERVICE STATIONS
        1,395

MISCELLANEOUS
Antique and Secondhand Stores	17,170
Book and Stationery Stores	28,580
Drugstores	4,268
Florists	13,531
Fuel Oil Dealers	25,000
Garden Supply Stores	65,000
Gift, Novelty Shops	26,000
Hobby, Toy, and Game Shops	61,000
Jewelry Stores	13,400
Optical Goods Stores	62,800
Sporting Goods Stores	27,000

From "Starting and Managing a Small Business of Your Own," 1973, Small Business Administration, Washington, D.C.

C. SITE-LOCATION

1. Define your number of inhabitants per store.
2. Locate several sites/locations that will match your inhabitants per store
3. Define population and it's growth potential
4. Define local ordinances and zoning regulations that you will need in order to start your type of business
5. Define your trading area and all competitors in your trading area
6. Define parking need, for your kind of business
7. Define special needs, etc., lighting, heating, ventilation
8. Define rental cost of site/location
9. Define why customers will come to your site/location
10. Define the future of your site/location as to population growth
11. Define your space needs and match with site/location selection
12. Define the image of your business and make sure it matches your site/location

D. CHOOSE PROPER ORGANIZATION

SINGLE PROPRIETORSHIP ADVANTAGES
1. Easy to Start
2. Low Start-up Cost
3. Complete Control, All Business Decisions
4. Sole Owner of All Profits
5. Limited Regulations
6. Freedom of Operation

SINGLE PROPRIETORSHIPS DISADVANTAGES
1. Unlimited Liability
2. Lack of Continuity
3. Difficulty in Raising Capital
4. Difficulty in Management Control

PARTNERSHIP ADVANTAGES
1. Legal Entity
2. Low Start-up Cost
3. Greater Management Control
4. Greater Capital Supply
5. Tax Advantage

PARTNERSHIP DISADVANTAGES
1. Unlimited Liability
2. Lack of Continuity
3. Difficulty in Management Control
4. Divided Profits
5. Difficulty in Raising Capital

CORPORATION ADVANTAGES
1. Limited Liability
2. Legal Entity
3. Increase Capital Advantage
4. Increase Management Control and Unlimited Life
5. Increase Continuity/Unlimited Life
6. Increase Ease of Ownership Transfer

CORPORATION DISADVANTAGES
1. Unlimited Regulations
2. Increase Start-up Cost
3. Double Taxation
4. Chapter Restrictions
5. Increase Recordkeeping Forms

E. ESTIMATE START-UP COSTS

1. Fixtures and Equipment $_____
2. Building & Land if Needed $_____
3. Store, and/or Office Supplies $_____
4. Remodeling and Decorating $_____
5. Deposits on Utilities $_____
6. Insurance $_____
7. Installation of Fixtures $_____
8. Legal Fees $_____
9. Professional Fees $_____
10. Telephone $_____
11. Rental $_____
12. Salaries and Wages $_____

13. Inventory if Retailing $_____
14. Licenses and Permits $_____
15. Advertising and Promotion $_____

TOTAL Estimated Start-up Cost $_____

F. HOW TO PREPARE AN INCOME STATEMENT

The income statement shows the income received and the expenses incurred over a period of time. Income received (sales) comes essentially from the sales of the merchandise or service which your business is formed to sell. Expenses incurred are the expired costs that have been incurred during the same period of time.

PLAN A BUDGETED INCOME STATEMENT FOR ONE YEAR
1. Project Total Sales
2. Estimate Total Expenditures
3. Example Listed Below for Income Statement

NAME OF BUSINESS
INCOME STATEMENT
DATE 12 MONTH

		1	2	3	4	5	6	7	8	9	10	11	12
SALES													
Cost of Sales	100%												
Gross Profit	48%												
EXPENDITURE													
Rent Expense	4%												
Supplies Expense	2%												
Wages & Salaries	18%												
Utilities	2%												
Insurance	1%												
Depreciation	2%												
Interest	1%												
Misc. Expense	2%												
NET PROFIT	16%												

G. HOW TO PREPARE A BALANCE SHEET

The balance sheet shows the assets, liabilities and owner's net worth in a business as of a given date. Assets are the items owned by your business, including both physical items and claims against others. Liabilities are the amounts owed to others, the creditors of the firm. Net worth or owner's equity is the owner's claim to the assets after liabilities are accounted for.

A BUDGETED BALANCE SHEET FOR ONE YEAR

1. List all your business property at their cost to you: These are your assets.

2. List all debts, or what your business owes on all your property. These are your liabilities.

3. Take your total property balance (Assets), and subtract the total amount you owe (Liabilities). The balance is what you own in your business called (Owner's equity).

4. Add Total Liabilities (2)
   Total Owner's Equity (3)

5. Listed on the next page is an example of a balance sheet.

NAME OF BUSINESS
BALANCE SHEET
DATE

ASSETS

CURRENT ASSETS:
Cash _____
Accounts Receivable _____
Merchandise Inventories _____

TOTAL CURRENT ASSETS _____

FIXED ASSETS:
Land _____
Building _____
Equipment _____

TOTAL FIXED ASSETS _____

TOTAL ASSETS 1. _____

LIABILITIES

CURRENT LIABILITIES:
Accounts Payable
Note Payable
Payroll Taxes Payable

TOTAL CURRENT LIABILITIES _____

LONG-TERM LIABILITIES:
Mortgage Payable _____
Long Term Note _____

TOTAL LONG TERM LIABILITIES _____
TOTAL LIABILITIES 2. _____

OWNER'S EQUITY

PROPRIETOR'S CAPITAL 3. _____

TOTAL LIABILITIES & OWNER'S EQUITY 2.&3. _____

H. MARKET YOUR BUSINESS
1. Define Your Market
   a. Type of Customers
   b. Age, Income, Occupation of your Customers
   c. Type of Trading Area

2. Promotion of Your Business
   a. Advertising
   b. Setting your Image

3. Customer Policy Plan
   a. Develop a Customer Profile
   b. Customer Services
   c. Customer Needs

4. Pricing Your Products/Services
   a. Know all your Costs
   b. Know your Profit Margin
   c. Know your Competitor's Price
   d. Know what Return you want on your Investment

5. Sales Promotion
   a. Coupons
   b. Contests
   c. Displays
   d. Demonstrations
   e. Giveaways
   f. Banners

6. Public Relations

a. Newspaper Article
b. Radio Promotion
c. Contact with your Trade Association
d. T.V. Promotion

7. Segmentation of your Market
   a. Age   d. Location
   b. Occupation   e. Education
   c. Income   f. Hobbies

I. GETTING THE WORK DONE, MANAGEMENT

1. Define your objective for starting your business.
2. Define your goals for profit growth for the first three years.
3. Develop an organization chart of your business.

SAMPLE OF AN ORGANIZATION CHART

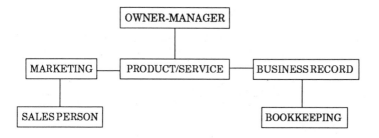

87

4. Define your personal needs.
   1. Hiring proper employees
   2. Training employees
   3. Motivation

5. Define all responsibility for each person in your business.

6. Define all authority.
   1. Who will hire and fire?
   2. Who will select and train all personnel?
   3. Who will keep the important records as to inventory, purchasing, sales records, cash records, etc.?

7. Define all laws and regulations that will be requirements for operating your business.

8. Review all duties and tasks with all your employees.

9. Write a summary of all the important tasks that you want to complete in your first year in business.

J. SUMMARIES OF YOUR BUSINESS PLAN

1. Listed on the next page is an outline of a standard business plan.

NAME OF BUSINESS
BUSINESS PLAN
DATE

I. Define your business
    a. Name all principals
    b. Address and phone number

II. Define your products or services

III. Define your market

IV. Define your site or location

V. Advertising Plan
    a. Budget
    b. Media

VI. Chart of Start-up cost

VII. Worksheet of Income Statement

VIII. Worksheet of Balance Sheet
    a. Assets (Property)
    b. Liabilities (Debts)
    c. Capital (Owner's Equity)

IX. Personnel Outline
    a. Number of Employees
    b. Staffing & Training

X. Management Organization
    a. Organization Chart
    b. Job Profile
    c. Evaluation Policy

XI. Special Statement
    a. Cash Flow
    b. Three Year Sales Schedule
    c. Three Year Expense Schedule

K. SUMMARY OF START-UP GUIDE

1. Contact your State Commerce Department for guidelines in starting your business.

2. Contact your City/County Clerk for guidelines in starting your business.

3. Contact all other Governmental Centers that will furnish you all the legal regulations and tax laws that will effect your business.
   1. State Government
   2. Internal Revenue Service
   3. State Employment Security Commission
   4. Department of Treasury
   5. City Governmental Units
      a. Fire
      b. Police
      c. Zoning
      d. Building Permits
      e. Health
      f. Water & Sewage

4. Township Government
   1. Local Legal Requirement
   2. Local Taxes
   3. Local Health Permits
   4. Local Zoning Laws

L. REFERENCE MATERIALS FOR STARTING YOUR BUSINESS

1. Contact the Small Business Administration at: P.O. Box 30 Denver, Colorado 80201-0030 for the following booklets.

   A. Management Aids Number MP12
      Title: Checklist For Going Into Business
   B. Management Aids Number MP6
      Title: Planning and Goal Setting For Business
   C. Management Aids Number FM9
      Title: Sound Cash Management
   D. Management Aids Number FM1
      Title: The A.B.C.'s of Borrowing
   E. Management Aids Number FM11
      Title: Break-even Analysis
   F. Management Aids Number MP11
      Title: Business Plan For Service Firms
   G. Management Aids Number MP9
      Title: Business Plans for Retail Firms

BIBLIOGRAPHY

Anderson, R., and Dunkelberg, J., *Entrepreneurship: Starting A New Business,* New York, Harper and Row, 1990.

Archer, M., and White, J., *Starting and Managing Your Own Business,* Cost and Management, 1979, page 40.

Baty, Gordon B, *Entrepreneurship: Playing to Win,* Reston, VA: Reston Publishing Company, 1974.

Dailey, Charles, *Entrepreneurial Management,* New York: McGraw Hill., 1971.

Hansen, James, *Guide to Buying or Selling a Business,* Englewood Cliffs, NJ: Prentice Hall Publishers, 1975.

Kuehl, C., and Lambing, P., *Small Business: Planning and Management,* CBS College Publishing, New York, 1987.

Kuratko, D., and Hodgetts, R., *Entrepreneurship: A Contemporary Approach,* New York: Holt, Rinehart, and Winston, Inc. Saunders College Publishing, 1989.

Liles, Patrick, *New Business Ventures and the Entrepreneur,* Homewood, IL: Richard D. Irwin Publishers, 1974.

Mancuso, Joseph, *Fun and Guts—The Entrepreneur's Philosophy,* Reading, MA: Addison Wesley Publishers, 1973.

Myer, John, *Accounting for Non-Accountants,* New York: Hawthorne Books, 1977.

Prather, Charles, and West, James, *Financing Business Firms,* Homewood IL: Richard D. Irwin Publishers, 1971.

Pyle, William, and White, *Fundamental Accounting Principles,* Homewood, IL: Richard D. Irwin Publishers, 1975.

Wayne, William, *How to Succeed in Business When the Chips Are Down,* New York: McGraw Hill Publishers, 1979.

INDEX

LIST OF BUSINESS PLANS

Each business plan is an easy to read, step-by-step approach
to starting and managing your special business.
Cost only $9.95 each.

Check

1. How To Start and Manage An
   Apparel Store Business ☐

2. How To Start and Manage A Word
   Processing Service Business ☐

3. How To Start and Manage
   A Garden Center Business ☐

4. How To Start and Manage
   A Hair Styling Shop Business ☐

5. How To Start and Manage
   A Bicycle Shop Business ☐

6. How To Start and Manage
   A Travel Agency Business ☐

7. How To Start and Manage
   An Answering Service Business ☐

8. How To Start and Manage
   A Health Spa Business ☐

9. How To Start and Manage
   A Restaurant Business ☐

Check

10. How To Start and Manage
    A Specialty Food Store Business ☐

11. How To Start and Manage
    A Welding Business ☐

12. How To Start and Manage
    A Day Care Service Business ☐

13. How To Start and Manage
    A Flower and Plant Store Business ☐

14. How To Start and Manage
    A Construction Electrician Business ☐

15. How To Start and Manage
    A Housecleaning Service Business ☐

16. How To Start and Manage
    A Nursing Service Business ☐

17. How To Start and Manage A
    Bookkeeping Service Business ☐

18. How To Start and Manage A
    Secretarial Service Business ☐

TO ORDER BUSINESS PLANS

Please Remit To:

LEWIS AND RENN ASSOCIATES
10315 HARMONY DRIVE
INTERLOCHEN, MICHIGAN 49643

Business Guide # _____ Title _____

Business Guide # _____ Title _____

Business Guide _____

Name _____   Plus 4% Sales Tax _____

Address _____ U.S. Shipping & Postage __$1.00__

City _____   Total _____

State _____ Zip _____